Rochester's Fa

arranged for medium voice and piano

by

Michael Nyman

CHESTER MUSIC

CH74360
ISBN 978-1-84772-762-6

Music setting by Nicholas Hare and Jon Bunker

© 2008 Chester Music Ltd

Published in Great Britain by Chester Music Limited
(Part of The Music Sales Group)
Head office:
14–15, Berners Street,
LondonW1T 3LJ
England

Tel +44 (0)20 7612 7400
Fax +44 (0)20 7612 7549

Sales and hire:
Music Sales Distribution Centre,
Newmarket Road,
Bury St. Edmunds IP33 3YB
Suffolk
England

Tel +44 (0)1284 702600
Fax +44 (0)1284 768301

www.chesternovello.com

All Rights Reserved
Printed in Great Britain
No part of this publication may be copied or reproduced
in any form or by any means without the prior permission
of Chester Music Limited

ROCHESTER'S FAREWELL